Beautiful Trauma

by

Sharon Harris

Sharon Harris
ANAHEIM, CA 92806

© 2021

This book is dedicated to my sister. Without her I couldn't have gotten this done. Even though I had to bug the crap out of her to get her help, she came through and contributed in a way that only an annoying little sister can. LOL I love you but it's true! Thank you, Author Ann Harris, let's get your books published.

Table of Contents

Innocence .... Page 10

A Young Girls Dream .... Page 11

***Molested... Page 12

Fantasy Life .... Page 13

Self-Hate.. Page 14

Fantasy Love... Page 15

First Love .... Page 16

Fading Love... Page 17

Forever Love .... Page 18

Abusive Love... Page 19

Not Love .... Page 20

Spiraling .... Page 21

Trauma Bond.. Page 22

Abuse .... Page 23

Lost .... Page 24

***Heart Sick .... Page 25

Suicidal Thoughts .... Page 26

Depression .... Page 27

Deciding .... Page 28

One Day .... Page 29

Empowerment .... Page 30

Manifest Love .... Page 31

Found Love .... Page 32

Finally .... Page 33

Love .... Page 34

***Womb .... Page 35

My God .... Page 36

Ending .... Page 37

Emotions .... Page 38

Breaking .... Page 39

Over You .... Page 40

Leaving .... Page 41

Gotta Go	Page 42
Who?	Page 43
Broken Mirror	Page 44
Drinking	Page 45
Who Am I?	Page 46
Learning To Love Me	Page 47
Consistency Is Key	Page 48
Struggling	Page 49
Reminiscing	Page 50
Seeking	Page 51
Grace	Page 52
It's Me	Page 53
Strategy	Page 55
Visualization	Page 56
True Self	Page 57
Conversations with The Mind	Page 58
I Am SHE	Page 59

INNOSENCE

One day, someday, I'll have all that I've dreamed of
One day, someday, I'll bask in the Divines true love
One day, someday, I'll be relaxing and writing on the beach
One day, someday, I'll host my very own writers retreat
One day, someday, traveling the world will be prioritized
One day, someday, I'll see that my dreams never died
One day, someday, I'll fall in love with my king
One day, someday, I'll know that he was also waiting and praying for me
One day, someday, I'll have grandkids of my own
One day, someday, I'll settle in a cozy place I call home
One day, someday, our nation will feel peace
One day, someday, people will realize that love is all we truly need
One day, someday, I'll pull those up who were left behind
One day, someday, I'll meditate until all of these things are mine

A YOUNG GIRLS DREAM

Eight years old, sitting alone outside
I love to watch the sun rise
Taking it all in
Gods vibrant colors, red, orange, yellow
Illuminating the sky
Bringing on the gorgeous sunshine
And actual warmth from way up high
I dream of one day becoming a successful entrepreneur
I know I'll make it out of the hood
I know I'll travel the world
One day, someday, I'll figure it all out

MOLESTED

You molest me; I'm an adolescent
You said I need to learn a lesson
You torment me with your silent aggression
Hush now. Don't ever make a confession
Years now my mind has been in oppression
The result of my emotions in suppression
Everyday my life is haunted by your impression
It's negatively affecting my indiscretion
I'm falling further and further into depression
Authentic joy separated, I have one expression
Contemplating; I have only one question
Will I ever see exponential progression?

FANTASY LIFE

Dying inside, I fantasize about all my hopes and dreams
What will I be like when I turn sixteen?
Or maybe when I'm twenty-three
Will I be the CEO of my own company?
Or climbing the ladder to build someone else's dream?
What if it's none of these?
Joining the military is also a thing
And maybe they'll have me traveling
I'll get married at twenty-five
And have my first child by twenty-nine
Life is good
I won't always be in the hood
I'll make it out
I have no doubt
I'll live the life of my dreams
It involves lots of shopping and traveling
Nothing can stop me
Living the good life is my destiny
I fantasize while dying inside

SELF-HATE

Daydreaming of my future life
I'm so tired of being in a constant fight
Frustrated with self-told lies
I'll get it right I say, next time
Here we are. Another year gone by
I torment myself with sweet, sweet lines
Telling myself, my destiny, I'll no longer deny
Turns out I've always got a new alibi
My self-worth I can no longer justify
Not sure why I even try
I let myself down every time
I don't love myself I've finally come to realize
Perhaps one day I will. In due time

FANTASY LOVE

What a beautiful night
You and I meeting for the first time
Sharing laughter, food and cocktails
Your company doesn't compare
I love the way you compliment me
Not just on my looks but personality
You recognize my inner beauty
That alone lets me know you're feeling me
We're quickly developing a beautiful friendship
I can't think of anything I want more than it
A smile sneaking up on me as I doze off tonight
I'll dream of me being yours and you being mine
Fantasizing until that day crosses our paths
I'll take solace in all the laughs we will have

FIRST LOVE

Meeting you is my dream coming true
These passionate feelings are brand new
Head over heels I'm falling for you
Each and every day I'm more and more in love with you
We can't spend enough time together
There aren't enough hours in the day
So, I'll dream of you when you're away
In your hands I place my heart
I love you so much, please don't crush it and tear me apart
I'm thinking a lifetime together
I believe we can brave the storms and inclement weather
A lifetime is not long enough to show you how much I care
For the rest of our lives I'll be in love with you baby I swear

FADING LOVE

I remember when you brought me flowers every week
Slowly, you slipped into emotionally abusing me
Forgetting who we were created to be
Disregarding my feelings, devaluing me

FOREVER LOVE?

Once upon a time
I thought we would grow old together
Coming out on top through all the storms and bad weather
My mind was quickly changed
When the blatant disrespect stayed the same
I love you still
Perhaps I always will...

ABUSIVE LOVE

With your fist in my face
I didn't sign up for this race
You're a liar, cheater and deceiver
Are you looking for an Emmy award
For the way that you performed
I am a pawn in your game
You're a fugazi, just lame
It took me a minute to figure out what you are
I never had a place in your heart
Now that I know, I release these scars
Your lack of empathy tore us apart
Once again, another bleeding heart

NOT LOVE

The sadness I feel each day
Won't let me continue to stay
Actions speak louder than words
Your actions have not gone unheard
Which is why I've been dying inside
But I have to snap out of it and regain control of my life
It saddens me even more
That you are attracted to filthy whores
We never really stood a chance
It's always been one sided in attempts to make this thing last
I hate that I allowed you to take over my life
I changed all of my plans to make things with you alright
How could you be so cruel
To continue all this time playing me for a fool
I lost myself in you
But I'm over it now, we're finally through

SPIRALING

Depression got a hold of me
Took control of me
Spiraling downhill
Quicker than I can prepare my next meal
Sunlight creeping in through the blinds
I prefer the darkness at this time
Drinking my sorrows away
Elated by another lonely day
Shut up in my room
No cleaning today, I'm through
Lying in bed
Covers over my head
Paralyzed
Alone and ready to die

TRAUMA BOND

Use me and abuse me.
Torment me with your lies
If I could take it all back, I would
I would say, not one more time
Will I allow you to crush my heart, tearing it in pieces
Back and forth
Your actions don't match your words
I can't take anymore
You leave me all alone crying here on the floor
You went and ran to your little whore
She has no self esteem
But you chose her over me

ABUSE

Clocks thrown and thoughts un-consoled
Bringing up his lies just one more time.
How can I say I already forgave.
It's not true. I'm all in his face.
He lied, cheated and stole
Looking me in the eyes with his toxic soul.
The Devil showed.
Was the torment worth my time?
When all I had to do was realize.
Every Battle is not mine to fight.
This could have been prevented before the next day showed its peaking light.
Quit thinking about how my life is a mess.
When all I had to do was say less.

HEARTSICK

No way was I prepared to take care of another life
I was barely able to fund mine
I immediately decided the Devil was a lie
Having a baby by that man didn't feel right
I just had to end your life
Lying on that cold table I couldn't help but cry
Now the deed is done
But what have I really won?
The seed I was blessed to conceive
I just can't believe
I sentenced a part of me to death
Flipped the switch before you had the opportunity to take your first breath
My heart shattered
It's all my fault you were unduly battered
I'm sorry I caused us so much pain
All because of my selfish brain
I still think of you each day
How big you'd probably be
The loving bond between you and me
All I'm left with is my imagination
And the guilt lingering from that occasion
If I could do it all over again, I would choose you
No matter what I'd have to endure
You'll always be in my heart
Right next to my personal dart

LOST

One day someday, is getting harder to believe
One day today, my dreams are slipping away from me
Lost in despair, how do I proceed?

SUICIDAL THOUGHTS

I have an overwhelming urge to cry
Please don't ask me why
It stems from depression. Got me feeling like I want to die
Sadness, anger, regrets and darkness overtaking my once happy life
I smile and say Hi but please understand it's all a lie
I feel worthless deep down inside
I cut myself in hopes the pain will suffice
Help me, I'm truly dying. My life I can't justify
Pretending is just too much. I'm unsatisfied
I'm all out of energy to keep up the fight
No more butterflies and blue skies. I'm ready to take my life
Turning off all the lights, I'm seeking permanent peace. Goodbye…

DEPRESSION

Downing a bottle of wine each night
To hide my feelings that are in plain sight
Ending the night feeling lonely and sad
It's only adding calories to my diet; retract
The weight I'm eager to lose
But depression has me eating like a fool
What I wouldn't do to be in your arms
It hurts because I've pushed you far
Far away from me
I can't let your love engage me
And trap me with your caress
God, I am such a mess

DECIDING

The life I want to live seems farfetched. I can't lie
It's going to take major sacrifice
Do you think I should roll the dice?
Maybe give it another try?
It's been haunting me day and night
Like a King in battle, I diligently put up a fight
But like a crisp new bill, I'm tryna start a new life
Picture me living in a brand-new paradise
I think I'll hold on real tight
To the thoughts and desires invading my sight
These genuine thoughts sincerely have me mesmerized!
Imagine each day filled with sunshine!
It gives me a tingly feeling deep down inside
This is the type of feeling I think I can live with for the rest of my life.

ONE DAY

One day, some day, I see that my dreams never died
One day, today, I'll meditate until all of these things are mine

EMPOWERMENT

From day to day the sun rises and shines
I get up early to get on my grind
Praying, fasting, having conversations with the Divine
Expressing my innermost feelings. Why bother to lie?
I confide in Him that dreams never die
Looking in the mirror, I simply want to cry
I was created with purpose that's drowning by self sabotage.
I'm creating my own demise
This is not something I freely advertise
But looking myself in the eye, I cannot deny
I truly need help so I can stabilize
As intelligent as I am, my actions are unwise
It's never too late now that I recognize...

MANIFEST LOVE

I can't wait to say I love you
And for our hearts to meet too
I dream of the day
We experience ecstasy and no more pain
When love is in the air
I won't say my past was unfair
I'll know it was all worth the ups and downs
To be genuinely happy with you starting now

FOUND LOVE

What a beautiful autumn day
A mix of both sunshine and rain
What do you think darling of you and I going on a date?
It's still early so we won't need to be out to late
What's the time? Let's catch a matinee
I think there's a new movie playing at the theater down by the lake
Grab the orange juice and I'll stop for some champagne
In the back of my truck at the drive-in we can parlay
Hopefully this rain stops without further delay
This could be the start of a perfect day
I love being off on Fridays
It's my favorite day and I just got paid
I can even grab us some Mary Jane
It'll help us feel relaxed, It really is a great escape
So are you down to celebrate with me on this holiday?
I actually still own that old baby making cassette tape
I could really use this short but fun get away
I hope this rain stops. Let us pray
It's a good thing we live on faith
Otherwise the rain could potentially ruin our entire day
Baby, are you ready to celebrate?
And take advantage of this holiday?
Ready to behave in a reckless way?
Just kidding. We won't do anything that could potentially get us detained.
We'll have a blast on our little escapade.
It's an easy decision. No need to hesitate
Just say yes so we can start this amazingly unforgettable day.

FINALLY

One day, this day, I know that he was waiting and praying for me
One day, today, I've finally met my king

LOVE

I am so in love with you
I have been since the very first day I met you
Such an intense bond
I realized when the sun came up and presented dawn
I love your laugh
And how you hold my hand
Your gentle kisses
I'm happy to be your Mrs.
My twin flame
A concept that is new but I accept it just the same
Many flames don't last
But us, we will defy the forecast
Over the years our love will grow
This is something that deep down I know
You're a part of me and I'm a part of you
Together in love, a family we will accrue
Meeting our son is something I am overjoyed to do
You have my heart. I hope you always know that I love you

WOMB

To my unborn son
I'm so grateful to finally share with you my unconditional love
I've dreamed of you for years
Your angelic face will bring me to tears
I want you more than you'll ever know
Smiling at the thought of the day I can finally hold,
Hold you in my arms
Protect you from imminent harm
Count your little toes
Your sweet innocence smells sweeter than any cologne
To my unborn son
My physical love for you has just begun
I'm feeling like a winner
My grin can't possibly get any bigger
I've waited for you for so long
Today I'm singing any and every love song
My heart is overflowing with joy
And that's all because of you, my baby boy

MY GOD

I feel like I might die
Just tell me God, Why?
Why do I deserve all this pain inside?
Why did you let my baby die?
Before he had the chance to experience life
Not only is it my unborn son I can't hold
But my husband is out living life solo
Tell me what I'm supposed to do
Today my life is brand new
Forcing me to realize
That right before my very eyes
My dreams have withered and died

ENDING

My twin flame
A concept that will never be the same
Our flame didn't last
I never foresaw the overcast
All my love I'm sending
Yet, our love is still ending

EMOTIONS

I want to write
Or even talk
But to who?
If someone only knew
My emotions are in overflow
I can't keep control
I'm crying inside
Every minute the tears threaten to overflow
But I keep a smile on my face
If anyone asks I lie and say I'm doing okay
It's just not true
Who cares enough to really know the truth?
Look into my eyes
They can't hide the lie
My heart is broken in more pieces than two
I just wish someone actually knew

BREAKING

It's like my Pandora station knows I'm sad as fuck
Playing all these sappy songs like, Damn what's up?
My Instagram is blowing up
With poems of tragically sad romances. What in the actual fuck?
Can I be lonely
By my damn self only?
I don't need comments coming that are phony
I'm so damn sad and truly lonely
My best friend isn't ready for me
My heart is broken in ten trillion pieces
Forever alone should be my motto
It's not natural to still stand here solo
But here I am one more time all alone so,
Say a little prayer for me
Because my heart is literally fucking breaking

OVER YOU

One day someday I'll be done with your false alibis
One day someday, the life I choose will be mine

LEAVING?

Stop with the lies
You've crushed my heart one to many times
Suddenly I should believe you?
Because you said I'm sorry and I love you?
Please put the crack pipe down
Clearly your head is in the clouds
Life is much more complicated than that
The world doesn't revolve around you jack
Put yourself in my shoes for once
No. Actually think about all you've done
Would you take me back?
After doing all of that?
No, you would not
Why is my heart not exempt from your plot?
Although, I still love you
We have to move on as two
My heart yearns for more
And it hurts me to my core
But in learning to love all of me
It's best we remain apart. Don't you agree?

GOTTA GO

I've been grieving the death of my best friend
With death so sudden
I can't continue to pretend
That we can still be something
Some pain lasts a lifetime
Time does not heal all wounds
The pain won't always subside
A void forever as my heart is being consumed
When you cross my mind, I get angry and want to cry
I've been missing you so much
Then I'm reminded why
Your love wasn't only for me, another you touched
Piercing my heart with needles
Each time you decided to lie
Even when our son didn't make it into this life
It's clear, you will never be only mine
The hurt is much worse than a literal death
I never knew such pain could manifest
Repeatedly opened up, unglued
I'm staying away now, I gotta recoup

WHO?

One day, someday I'll choose the life of my dreams
One day, someday I'll finally choose me

BROKEN MIRROR

I can't see out of the rear view
The glass shattered right along with you
Only fragments of the past
Pieces of the love we had
I can't see myself clearly
My face distorted; it's not the real me
I'm picking up the pieces
Trying not to cut myself deeper
Can I glue it back together?
I'm under a lot of pressure?
The mirror is broken now
How do I turn this frown upside down
Shattered is my mind, body and soul
How do I pick up the pieces and reload
When I can't see clearly
Who is the real me?

DRINKING

All these lonely nights
I spend alone drinking wine
Netflix is running out of heartbreak movies
Crying alone, I miss loving you, truly
No friend or confidant to offer comfort
Have they blocked or deleted my number?
Or am I alone because I pushed them all away?
Pathetically here alone on another Monday
Is anyone left to offer some insight?
Here I am experiencing more lonely nights

WHO AM I?

Sitting here feeling so sad
Trying not to think about the chap
Who causes these tears to flow
I'm better without him and that's a fact
I just need to work on realigning and getting back
To the woman I was created to be
Without him I rock because I am SHE

LEARNING TO LOVE ME

Each day I make time to meditate
It's conducive in keeping me sane
Connecting with my higher self
Thank you for giving me what's best for my health
Learning more and more to appreciate the subtle blessings all around
Birds chirping, cars driving, hearing the winds howl
Everything is happening for me
I'm grateful for all that I see
Life experiences are a teacher indeed
How I respond to life lessons can increase my peace
With my future in mind
I'm unstoppable this time
It's already done
The process of manifesting has just begun
Embracing all this life has to offer me
I take a step back to smell the flowers
And envision my life
It's so close in my sight

CONSISTENCY IS KEY

I'm on a mission
It requires me to be consistent
With my hopes and dreams
And everything I believe
I've seen my future life in my sleep
Absolutely peaceful and serene
Consistency is key
I'll achieve all the things
I've always seen in daydreams

STRUGGLING

Daydreaming of my future life
I'm so tired of being in a constant fight
Frustrated with self-told lies
I'll get it right I say, next time
Here we are, another year gone by
I torment myself with sweet, sweet lines
Telling myself, my destiny, I'll no longer deny
Turns out I've always got a new alibi
My self-worth I can no longer justify
Not sure why I even try
I let myself down every time
I don't love myself I've finally come to realize
Perhaps one day I will, in due time
The life I want to live seems farfetched. I can't lie
It's going to take major sacrifice
Do you think I should roll the dice?
Maybe give it another try?
It's been haunting me day and night
Like a king in battle, I diligently put up a fight
But like a crisp new bill, I'm tryna start a new life
Picture me living in a brand-new paradise
I think I'll hold on real tight
To the thoughts and desires invading my sight
These beautiful thoughts genuinely have me mesmerized
Imagine each day filled with sunshine
It gives me a tingly feeling deep down inside
This is the type of feeling I think I can live with for the rest of my life.

REMINISCING

Back in the day I had a survivor's mentality
My mind raced with intangible things, my reality
There has got to be more out there and better for me
It was so farfetched. A dream I'd never see
People don't make it out the hood. That's a scary thing
A product of their environment. Don't fall prey to those dying dreams
It's a trap the government and world decreed
I can't sit around to be part of a dying breed
Follow those passions suppressed through years of lies and disbelief
Inhale, exhale, I need oxygen to proceed
Further illuminating my mind to who I was created to be

SEEKING

I'm looking for a new high
Something to help my mind
Escape reality of the days
Long drawn out and in a major haze
Turning to inner peace
I'm seeking within for the release
Torment and pain has me mentally drained
I can only be excited now for the new days
Days with sunshine, no clouds or rain
No more mental, emotional or physical pain
A new reality
Filled with love, joy and serenity

GRACE

Lord guide me to the light
By leading me to write
An author is who you created me to be
It is in you that I see my dreams
Vivid and clear
The images never disappear
I write what I see
It's like a movie to me
When shared with the world
It will uncover those tarnished pearls
They were buried deep
And bruised both internal and externally
A bit of polishing will surely supersede
As your light reigns
In glory, the clouds and rain begin to fade
Forever changed
I am ever thankful for your grace

IT'S ME

What is stopping me from fulfilling my destiny?
My true purpose is much greater than you and me
There are people who need me to speak and plant a seed
It's so we can all come to fruition with our dreams
I know you don't understand it but we're actually a team
I'm a writer. I can embody your pain and spew it back out like acidic rain
I can't take this creative healing to my grave
When I know it can help so many through their pain
My words are like oxygen to a flame
They illuminate what's real and could possibly be your last day
Then I'll write back to electrify the debate
Letting you know that you too hun are super-duper great.
This is not just another ordinary day
I've given you a vision of your life play by play
You can now decide to choose your end game
So what's stopping me from creating the life I truly desire to lead?
Fear of failure and success? How stupid could I be?
What's really stopping me?
What if someone's life was truly dependent on me?
I should operate as if it is. I won't lose anything
This new found revelation makes me want to sing
I've always know I was created to live the life of my dreams
It's time for me to get off of my seat
Time for me to rethink some things
Develop a winning strategy
I'm ready to defeat the loser in me
The one who is scared of things unseen
Time to get organized and clear on the person I want to be
The multi-millionaire lady I see in daydreams

Knowing is half the battle and now I know, what's stopping me has always been me...

STRATEGY

One day someday, I'll rethink some things
One day, today I'm developing a winning strategy

VISUALIZATION

I'm just tryna live my best life!
That's the statement I made to my tribe
Getting up when the sun shines
And going to bed with the moonlight
I'm gonna live my best life
No more denying the fire inside
Let's be real now, it's never gonna die
It excites me to see beautiful rays of sunshine
With ocean waters dripping down my spine
The sun dancing on my skin feels so, so divine
The time on my watch says it's now almost five
Before dinner, I'll indulge, a glass of red wine
With my glass and a hammock you'll find me near the coastline
Imagine all of this done by perfect design
Imagine none of this costing a dime
Imagine having children visiting all of the time
Imagine my novels listed as best sellers in the New York Time
Imagine me always laughing and having a good time
Cooking with my husband right there by my side
Traveling the world, the A team is he and I
We make a power couple with our talents combined
I told y'all already, I'm just tryna live my best life!
Studying cultures and food. I gain so much insight!
It brings me joy to create a new dish that we all love and not just like!
Flipping traditional cuisines, everyone will want to try
I see my future, so close in my sight
Picture me like this every day, just living my best life!

True Self

There's this thing I toy with called spirituality
I honestly believe it's been a true blessing to me
Manifesting my hopes, desires and dreams
What an amazing time to be alive you see
My friends don't understand it
They wonder if I'm being underhanded
But they know my heart holds no malice
I'm just tryna save the world single handed
I know some people can't stand it
Why? I'm not even fully established
This is a lifelong journey. I didn't pre plan it
I have a mission to lead with intention
I hope someone will actually listen

Conversations with The Mind

I be having conversations with the Divine
Sometimes aloud but usually in my mind
We're on the same wavelength because you live in me
As a part of me. We are one
These words are all about us
Working out the kinks
Trying to rethink
Remix. Resist the same flow
Stepping into times unknown
I'm done putting on a show
I can only be me so I'm definitely working toward developing unconditional love for me
I deserve all of the finest things
All that I believed in dreams

I AM SHE

I am SHE
Strong and bright like the noonday sun
I am SHE
Glowing so radiantly
I am SHE
Once feeling defeated, I got up and saw the reflection of a Queen
I am SHE
Staring in the mirror, the reflection I saw was me
I am SHE
The daughter of the most high King
I am SHE
Clothed from head to toe in royalty
I am SHE
From the torments of the night, I've been made free
I am SHE
Peace and prosperity I declared over me
I am SHE
Heir to the throne of our majesty
I am SHE
Mother, friend and businesswoman balancing my family's needs
I am SHE
Living my life, I've changed my style of fight
I am SHE
I get down on my knees and give it all to my savior and King
I am SHE
He said, "Abide in me"
I am SHE
Peace owing through me like the calming waves of the Caribbean Sea
I am SHE
No one can keep me from my destiny

I am SHE
Smile princess, you also are me
And we are SHE